Brahms

Waltz in A-flat (Op.39, No.15)

Cover photography: Fotolia.

Project editor: Peter Pickow.

Order No. AM948706
International Standard Book Number: 0.8256.1738.3

Exclusive Distributors:
Music Sales Corporation
180 Madison Avenue, 24th Floor, New York NY 10016, USA.
Music Sales Limited
Distribution Centre, Newmarket Road, Bury St Edmunds, Suffolk IP33 3YB, UK.
Music Sales Pty Limited
Units 3-4, 17 Willfox Street, Condell Park, NSW 2200, Australia.

Printed in the EU.

Amsco Publications
New York / London / Paris / Sydney / Copenhagen / Berlin / Madrid / Hong Kong / Tokyo

Waltz in A-flat

Op.39, No.15

Johannes Brahms